s e x

Scott Petty

Little Black Books: Sex
© Matthias Media 2010

Matthias Media
(St Matthias Press Ltd ACN 067 558 365)
PO Box 225
Kingsford NSW 2032
Australia
Telephone: (02) 9663 1478; international: +61-2-9663-1478
Facsimile: (02) 9663 3265; international: +61-2-9663-3265
Email: info@matthiasmedia.com.au
Internet: www.matthiasmedia.com.au

Matthias Media (USA)
Telephone: 724 964 8152; international: +1-724-964-8152
Facsimile: 724 964 8166; international: +1-724-964-8166
Email: sales@matthiasmedia.com
Internet: www.matthiasmedia.com

ISBN 978 1 921441 72 1

Cover design and typesetting by Matthias Media.

Contents

Introduction

Whenever I need to get the attention of the guys and girls in my youth group I just say the word 'sex'. Sometimes it makes the junior youth groupers giggle (they laugh at everything), but I know that this word cuts through every rowdy conversation that's going on, and the hall always falls deadly silent. That's because teenagers are interested in sex, and Christian teenagers are no exception. They're not necessarily all interested in having sex, but they are interested in knowing about sex and learning about sex.

In the chapters that follow we are going to look at designer sexuality, by which I just mean sex as it was designed by God, who invented sex in the beginning. We will cover the topics of marriage, Christian dating, homosexuality and pornography. It should be interesting. My hope is that by the end you will not only know what God thinks about designer sexuality, but will trust that what he says is good, and is for our good.

CHAPTER 1

Where to find the best sex

You are bombarded by sexual messages even more than you realize. And you probably realize it quite a lot. It is estimated that the average person is exposed to about 14,000 sexual messages per year (just under 40 a day), and less than 200 of those 14,000 advise caution or hesitation about sex.

The vast majority of these sexual messages promote some version of what we might call The Robbie Williams View of Sex. In 2006, Robbie Williams released a song called 'Sin Sin Sin'. It has a really catchy tune; the kind of song that you find yourself singing along to until you realize that he is talking about taking a random girl home for sex. That's pretty much what most of his songs are about. In the first verse of the song he says these interesting things:

> Don't let your eyes tell your brain you should feel ashamed.
> Everyone needs it baby and I feel the same

Didn't quite catch your name
Hush, hush, hush don't say a thing
Let's see what the night will bring
It might be everything.[1]

For Robbie Williams, sex is just a physical need. Just a physical need that everyone has. So don't feel ashamed about it, because it is just a physical need, like eating. That's pretty much all it is—just physical—and it's not about relationship at all. He doesn't even know the girl he's going to have sex with; didn't quite catch her name. Doesn't matter though, says Robbie, let's just see what the night will bring—it could be everything. Probably not though, if he's honest, because if he doesn't even know the name of the woman he's sleeping with then it's hard to imagine how he will find a glimmer of love and life deep inside, which is what he hopes for in the song.

The whole point of the song is that casual sex is not sin sin sin, but just a normal physical need. He doesn't think he needs rescuing. In fact, he even says that a one-night stand—sex with a stranger—is just what Jesus would do. I'd like to see a Bible verse for that!

But before you start shaking your head, you have to understand

8

why this song became a hit. It's not just about the catchy tune that you cannot get out of your head. It's that Robbie Williams' lyrics pretty much sum up our society's view of sex. Sex is just a physical need to be met, and should be taken and given freely. I used to think that this was just the guy's view of sex, but some recent surveys suggest that over half of Australian women have made a 'booty call'—that is, calling a man they know for casual, non-committed sex—at least once. In other words, the Robbie Williams view is about as mainstream as the most popular TV shows. You can see it in teen dramas like *Neighbours*, in prime-time comedies such as *Just Shoot Me*, *Two and a Half Men* and *Will & Grace*, and in the highest-rating shows in the country, including *Desperate Housewives* and *Grey's Anatomy* (not to mention TV shows whose titles even focus on casual sex, like *Sex in the City* and *Californication*). It is more common than not for characters on TV to sleep with each other on the first date. That is the common view of sex. Not much more than a physical need.

Now you may already be guessing that I don't think a whole lot of The Robbie Williams View of Sex. And you'd be right. But what's the alternative? Maybe you're thinking that I am about to suggest that sex is sinful, and that you should STOP IT. Maybe you think that the only real alternative to The Robbie Williams View of Sex is The Ruth Smythers View of Sex. Here's a quote from Ruth Smythers' article, 'Instruction and Advice for the Young Bride':

> To the sensitive young woman who has had the benefits of proper upbringing, the wedding day is, ironically, both the happiest and most terrifying day of her life. On the positive side, there is the wedding itself, in which the bride is the central attraction in a beautiful and inspiring ceremony, symbolizing her triumph in securing a male to provide for all her needs for the rest of her life. On the negative side, there is the wedding night, during which the bride must pay the piper, so to speak, by facing for the first time the terrible experience of sex.
>
> At this point, dear reader, let me concede one shocking truth. Some young women actually anticipate the wedding night ordeal with curiosity and pleasure! Beware such an attitude! A selfish and sensual husband can easily take advantage of such a bride. One cardinal rule of marriage should never be forgotten: GIVE LITTLE, GIVE SELDOM, AND ABOVE ALL, GIVE GRUDGINGLY. Otherwise what could have been a proper marriage could become an orgy of sexual lust.

Now if you think this sounds too ridiculous to be true, you'd be right. This quote, supposedly written by a minister's wife in 1894, is one of those hoaxes that are spread so easily by the internet. It's an over-the-top send up of what is supposedly the 'Christian' approach to sex—that sex is dirty, distasteful, and only to be endured for the making of babies.

But perhaps this is not as ridiculous as it looks when it's put down in black and white, pen on paper, Ruth Smythers style. Young people who have grown up in the church, who have often been told that sex is something that Christians don't do, at least not until they're married, and who are constantly encouraged to be 'children of the light' who stand out from their non-Christian peers by their godly living, just might harbour negative views about sex. There's a decent chance that some young people, somewhere in their minds, think sex is somehow wrong, dirty or a no-go zone, even though they are probably at the same time fascinated by sex and intrigued by sexuality.

And if Ruth Smythers was the only alternative, I could understand why people might side with Robbie Williams.

Is there room for designer sexuality?

In light of the two options before us, that sex is either dirty or just physical, I want to offer a third alternative: that sex is a profound gift from God for our benefit. It is not dirty, because it is designed by God himself, who gives only good things (1 Tim 4:4). And it is not just physical, because God designed it to be intensely emotional and profoundly spiritual as well. The sex that God made is something very valuable and precious, and not worth cashing in too cheaply.

When I was 19, I had a real job that paid real money, at least more money than I had ever seen before. And one day I saw this black leather motorcycle jacket in a second-hand shop in a trendy part of town. I thought it was great—it was in good condition and looked pretty bad-boy—so I paid a couple of hundred dollars for it. The problem with motorcycle jackets is that they are only comfortable when you are in the "I'm riding a motorcycle" position, leaning forward, white-knuckling the handlebars. In other positions, it's not really that easy to move your arms. So I only ever wore this great jacket that I had paid hundreds of dollars for three times. I eventually took it to another second-hand shop, kind of an early 1990s equivalent to eBay, hoping to make most of that money back. But the shop would only give me $30. And stupidly I took it. I traded in something that was valuable way too cheaply. I reckon that's what many young people do with sex and their sexuality. They trade in something that is valuable and precious as though it was just something common, something cheap, something that's not worth much at all.

So you need to know why sex is worth not trading in too cheaply. And you need to know how to use your sexuality in line with the design of its creator, who is also our creator, the living and true God. To get to the point, I want to explain why it is worth the wait for marriage, for that is God's design for sex. Marriage is where to find the best sex.

Marriage is the place for the best sex

Straight up, it is clear from the Bible that marriage is the place for sex between human beings. By the way, when I say *sex*, I'm talking about intercourse, I'm talking about foreplay, I'm talking about oral sex. If you think anything looks or sounds or smells like sex, it most likely is, and that's what I'm talking about. When the Bible talks about the first marriage—between Adam and Eve in Genesis 2—it says this:

So the man gave names to all the livestock, the birds of the air and all the beasts of the field. But for Adam no suitable helper was found. So the LORD God caused the man to fall into a deep sleep; and while he was sleeping, he took one of the man's ribs and closed up the place with flesh. Then the LORD God made a woman from the rib he had taken out of the man, and he brought her to the man.

The man said,

> "This is now bone of my bones
>   and flesh of my flesh;
> she shall be called 'woman',
>   for she was taken out of man."

For this reason a man will leave his father and mother and be united to his wife, and they will become one flesh.

The man and his wife were both naked, and they felt no shame. (Gen 2:20-25)

So here are a few quick things about marriage that we learn from this first marriage between Adam and Eve.

Firstly, man and woman are built for each other. The animals are not the answer to the man's loneliness, because no suitable helper can be found from among them. Giraffes are cool to look at, but not cool to be with for very long. God had to make something like a man but different from a man to find a companion for the man. Man and woman are built for each other.

Secondly, sex is intended to be used within a binding relationship. In these verses, that's defined as the point when a man and a woman leave their families and unite to become one flesh (Gen 2:24). It is the context of marriage, a relationship in which the man and the woman bind themselves to each other—the fancy Bible word for this is a 'covenant' relationship. It is not passionate relationship, not loving relationship, not even committed relationship, but covenantal marriage relationship—a relationship in which a new family unit is formed, where a man leaves his father and mother and unites (that means sexually) with his wife. That's what all the bone of my bones stuff is about. It's where the man says, "Together we are a new family". It is intentional and significant, not casual and loose. And what it basically means is that if you're not ready to leave Mum and Dad and home, you're not ready for sex.

Look at what Adam says to set up the covenant, the binding promise, with Eve. She is part of me, we are one. We belong, we are tied together. I will not separate from you. And that is why you will hear the minister say at weddings, "What God has joined together let not man separate". In a marriage, a man and a woman bind themselves to each other. Now it doesn't always work out right, because men and women are sinful, but that deep binding commitment of marriage is what sex was designed for. That also means it's the best sex, because that's where our designer God says it belongs. (Incidentally, research also bears this out. In their book, *The Case for Marriage*, Linda Waite and Maggie Gallagher show from extensive research that married people have more sex and better sex than unmarried people.[2])

When you see that sex is designed for this deep relationship, you realize that sex is not just a union—they will become united in one flesh—it's almost a *re*union. The woman was made from the man, and in sex they are once again joined. That's a level of deepness that Robbie Williams won't understand if he insists on sleeping with strangers. In marriage, a man and a woman become one flesh; they become a part of one another, bound together by love, expressed in the supremely powerful union of sex.

The third and last thing to say from Genesis 2 is that married sex is unashamedly good. I think marriage is under attack in our society. People see it as a boring, restrictive and passionless arrangement. In fact, when was the last time you saw some hot or romantic scene on TV that featured a married couple?

But in the first marriage, the man and woman are together, naked and unashamed. Sex didn't happen *after* the fall, as if it was what got them into trouble. On the contrary. They are united in marriage and sex as part of God's good creation. Not ridden by guilt and repressing themselves but unashamedly in love, unclothed, and into each other. Not passionless but passionate, not restrictive but committed, not boring but sexy. Hot, heterosexual, married sex.

And why wouldn't it be hot, because that's what sex is like when it's used the way it was designed to be used. Not just physical and certainly not dirty, but between a man and a woman who have bound themselves to each other under God for the long haul. That's always going to be better than just seeing what the night will bring in the vain hope for a glimmer of love. The Bible doesn't just command us to wait for marriage rather than trading in our sexuality cheaply. For those with ears to hear, it tells us why it's worth the wait; why it's deep and profound; and why marriage is the place for the best sex.

How do we wait well?

I hope that it has been clear enough that having a sexuality in line with God's design means waiting until marriage—a binding relationship—to explore sex and your sexuality. But what do you do in the meantime? I realize that waiting sounds unusual in our culture and society. We have a movie like *40 Days and 40 Nights*, which is about whether a guy can wait 40 days to have sex. Or *The 40-Year-Old Virgin* (what's with all the 40s!), where it is just ridiculously funny that a man could make it to 40 years of age without having sex. Hilarious! It is not really acceptable in our society to wait for sex. But we can wait; the question is how do we wait well.

The first way is to be careful of the ways we *think* about sex. This is going to be hard, because we hear tons of messages about sex every day, and virtually all of them fall well short of designer sexuality. Thinking righteously about sex, thinking God's way about sex, will mean training our minds to think differently from how the world wants us to think. For example, we want to see members of the opposite sex as people made in the image of God, with dignity and worth because God made them and Jesus died for them, rather than as objects of sexual desire or fantasy.

This means we have to be careful about what we fill our minds with, including the songs we sing along to, the books we read and the magazines we buy. Because guys are generally wired visually—we get turned on by what we see—Christian girls who love their brothers in Christ will not dress like one of Britney's back-up dancers, but will dress modestly like the New Testament says (1 Tim 2:9). But guys can help themselves by not *expecting* girls to dress like they have just starred in a music video. Gentlemen should also train themselves for godly thinking by not diving into internet porn. One of the main reasons that internet porn is bad for guys is that it trains them to think of women as just pieces of meat, as body parts separate from their personhood, and worth nothing more than what they can contribute to our sexual thoughts and actions. But women are created in the image of God! They are the only beings capable of being suitable companions for us as men. They deserve and desire more dignity than that. (Porn is so big an issue that there's a whole chapter devoted to it later on.)

Christian young people should also be careful with the shows they watch on TV. I'm not saying you should turn off any TV show that does not involve a cartoon Coyote trying to kill Road Runner. But some shows with strong sexual references and footage do nothing good for us, and the best thing we can do is to switch them off. Some shows—teen dramas, regular dramas like *Desperate Housewives* and *Grey's Anatomy*, even mainstream comedies—present a warped view of sexuality we should watch critically, if at all. This means that we watch them with our brains turned on and tuned into whether the show is glorifying designer sexuality or trading it in cheaply, so that we do not just take their view of sexuality on board as normal. The same applies to the songs we listen to. If we listen uncritically to songs that are all about having meaningless, lifeless, casual sexual experiences we can soon find ourselves adopting that view of sex as our own.

The way we talk to each other can also lead us either towards or away from designer sexuality. This doesn't mean that you can't talk about romances and relationships *at all*. But very often Christian youth are exactly the same as non-believers in the way they speak about members of the opposite sex. If we are going to think about the opposite sex in pure terms the answer cannot be to talk to them and about them with rogue conversation.

Touch is also an area in which to be cautious. Some touch is reserved for husbands and wives, including touching any area of the body that is normally covered by underwear (including breasts, bottoms and genital areas). It includes passionate kissing and long, lingering cuddles. I've seen couples fall pregnant from less physical contact than I have seen among 'friends' in Christian youth groups.

As well as these practical ideas to help you wait for marriage, it is also worth reminding yourself of some of the deep spiritual differences that being a child of God makes. Anyone can change their behaviour for a short period of time, but to wait well you need to know that you are not a helpless hostage of your hormones; you are made in the image of God. You are not a victim of our oversexed society; you are a new creation in Christ Jesus. And you don't have to resign yourself to being a young fool; with God's Holy Spirit, you have both the mind of Christ and his strength within you, and you have been set apart for godly living to his glory. I think it's good to remind yourself of these things often, as well as taking any necessary practical steps in regard to what we think, what we watch, how we talk and how we touch each other.

It's worth waiting well for marriage because marriage is where to find the best sex. After all, it's the place God designed for sex, where a man and a woman bind themselves to each other, where they form a new family, where they commit themselves to each other no matter what, where sex for them is not just a union but a reunion, where they become one. That is designer sex. Not just physical, and definitely not dirty.

CHAPTER 2

How far is too far: practical theology for dating relationships

It is just assumed in our society that if you have a boyfriend or girlfriend, you are entitled to sex. The question is not whether or not you should have sex, but how and how often. To prevent the spread of AIDS in Africa they teach people ABC: A for abstinence, B for *be* faithful and C for condoms. But you will probably never hear the word 'abstinence' (that is, not having sex) in sex education classes in our schools. Abstinence is an OK strategy for a whole continent like Africa, but for some reason it is not even mentioned as an option in Australian, British or American classrooms. And so once again the education system fails young people like you. Instead of giving you guidance about the choice of whether or not to have sex, education only gives advice about how to have 'safe' sex. You learn how to use a condom to prevent pregnancy and disease, but what they don't tell you is that sex can still be unsafe emotionally, psychologically and spiritually. Basically, the message is that as long as you use protection, you can dive right into sex with your boyfriend or girlfriend.

So far we have seen that sex is a good gift from God, and is designed to be enjoyed in the context of a binding covenant relationship that we call marriage. We have seen that the place for sex is between a man and a woman—we will talk about homosexuality in the next chapter—who have bound themselves to each other, under God, for the long haul. But if sex is designed for and reserved for marriage, what advice is there for people in boyfriend-girlfriend relationships? Are our sex education classes right? Do we go for it and just make sure it's safe? Is there any other guidance or guidelines? Any advice on boundaries? Or is it pretty much governed by what feels good?

Thankfully, there is some better advice from God about what is OK and not OK in dating relationships. 1 Thessalonians 4 is as good a place to begin as any. In this chapter, Christians are urged to live a holy life:

It is God's will that you should be sanctified: that you should avoid sexual immorality; that each of you should learn to control his own body in a way that is holy and honourable, not in passionate lust like the heathen, who do not know God; and that in this matter no one should wrong his brother or take advantage of him. The Lord will punish men for all such sins, as we have already told you and warned you. For God did not call us to be impure, but to live a holy life. (1 Thess 4:3-7)

It says that God wants us to be sanctified, and that God did not call us to be impure, but to live a holy life. But what does he mean by *sanctified* and *holy life*?

When we become Christians, God declares us to be right, to be just like Jesus in how he sees us. That is, we are *justified*. It's his decision. He decides to treat us as if we were sinless and perfect, just like Jesus. It's not that God doesn't really know all the mess that is going on down here in our lives. It's just that he decides, because of the death of Jesus in our place, to treat us or consider us as holy as Jesus was.

Sanctification is the other aspect of holiness that continues to pick away at our less than perfect selves, making us more like Jesus. It means growth in holiness towards Christlikeness as the Christian life continues. For example, I might go to a surgeon for a knee reconstruction because I'm getting old. The operation is a success and he says that my new knee is good. It's declared right. But at the time of the operation I haven't exercised for ages. I'm out of shape. So even though I have been declared 'fixed', I want my knee to be more and more like the perfect knee it was re-created to be. I want to exercise it, build the muscles around it, stretch them, see it get better and stronger the more time goes on. That's what it means here to be sanctified; it's an ongoing process in the Christian life towards the Jesus-like life we were created to live.

Avoid sexual immorality

So when the Apostle Paul tells the Thessalonian believers (and us) to live a holy life and be sanctified, he's telling them to become increasingly like Jesus in every aspect of life. Here it is especially in terms of our sexuality. And so the first way it says we ought to do that is by avoiding sexual immorality (v. 3). Some older Bibles translate this as "abstain from fornication". I reckon even the word 'fornication' sounds dirty.

What it means is that Christian people who are becoming increasingly like Jesus should avoid all kinds of immoral sexual practice. As we discovered in the last chapter, sexual immorality means all kinds of sex between partners who are not married to one another. That means sexual intercourse, foreplay and oral sex. Again, if it looks like sex or sounds like sex or smells like sex, it is sex, and it all counts. It's not very complicated. If you are married, avoid sex with someone you're not married to. If you are not married, avoid sex with everyone until you are married. If you are tempted by homosexuality, avoid sex with members of the same sex. If you are a lonely farmer, avoid sex with your animals (I only mention this because Leviticus 18 includes it among a number of other sexual perversions). And so on. If you want to know how to live a life pleasing to God, how to be sanctified, how to be pure, then avoid sexual immorality.

You need to notice carefully that it doesn't say avoid sex. It says avoid sexual immorality. God is not against sex. Why would he be, since he made it? And he doesn't want Christians to avoid sex if they are married. But he does want them all—married, unmarried, divorced, going out, lonely farmers, whatever—to avoid sexual immorality in all its forms. This might sound completely bizarre in our age where every hip-hopper, gangsta rapper, music video, TV drama, billboard and ad assumes that there's no such thing as sexual immorality, apart from unprotected sex. But avoiding sexual immorality remains God's radical and timeless word on this subject. Do not ignore it.

Learn to control your own body

The next part of 1 Thessalonians 4 says that each of us should "learn to control his own body in a way that is holy and honourable" (v. 4). Avoiding sexual immorality is a negative statement. Don't get me wrong, I think it's awesome advice—I'm just observing that it says, "Don't do this!" But learning to control your own body is a positive statement. It's saying, "Do this!"

And what we're positively to do is to control our own body. And I really like that it doesn't just say "control your own body". It says *learn* to control it, which means there is hope for those of us who think we can't control our own bodies. It is a learning process. As a 15-year-old boy, I remember thinking that the average tree looked pretty attractive. Anyone female and about my age I thought was complete dynamite. I thought I had no hope of controlling my body and nobody told me that I could. But the truth is that I could have started to control my body, because controlling your body is a learning process.

It would have been a learning process for the Thessalonian Christians who grew up living as heathens—which just means that they did not know or care about the living and true God. It was part of the heathen religious culture of the day to have sex with temple prostitutes; that was what dudes did as part of the church services in honour of the local idols—which is one way to make sure religion stays popular. The Thessalonians had to learn to change, to control their bodies. It was a learning process for them, and it will be for you, as you grow up surrounded not only by sexual messages and temptations, but also by the people who make those sexual messages and give themselves over to temptation. The good news is that it is actually possible to learn how to control your body. You start by reminding yourself often of who you are as a Christian: made in God's image, a new creation in Christ Jesus, set apart for righteousness and living for his glory. And you continue by putting practical steps in place that will help you avoid temptation.

Don't take advantage of each other

The third way to be sanctified or live a holy life in 1 Thessalonians 4 is that no-one should "wrong his brother or take advantage of him" (v. 6). 'Brother' here means 'fellow believer' rather than 'blood brother'. It's sort of like the way we use the word 'guys'. He's basically saying, "Come on guys, don't wrong each other and don't take advantage of one another".

How do we wrong each other or take advantage of each other today? We wrong each other or take advantage of each other if we are sexually immoral with someone, because we have led them to sin or stained their soul with our sin. There's no two ways about it. If we don't avoid sexual immorality but jump into it, which is what we most often feel like doing, then we take advantage of a fellow believer.

But we also wrong that person's future husband or their future wife. If we are sexually immoral with a brother or sister in Christ today, then we have taken something that belonged to that person's future husband; we have robbed that person's future wife of the innocence and purity of that moment when they first climb into bed together and enjoy good, earthy, passionate love as God created it to be. For that matter, we have robbed our own future husbands and wives as well. Sexual immorality might feel right at the time, but it's not. Christian young men should think of the Christian girls they know as the future wives of their Christian brothers, and treat them with purity as sisters. Christian girls should think of the Christian guys they know as the future husbands of their sisters, and treat them with respect as brothers.

So how far can I go?

"How far can I go?" is the question you're interested in, so let's get practical. I hope it's OK to say that young people can sometimes be like miniature Pharisees, always looking to draw lines about what is right and what is wrong so that they can go as close to that line as possible. But instead of talking about lines, let's talk practicalities.

There are stacks of ways that we can avoid sexual immorality, learn to control our own bodies, and not take advantage of one another. But let's start with ourselves. We can make an excellent start by shutting out some of those unhelpful sexual messages—by filtering what we listen to, what we watch and what we talk about (like we talked about in the last chapter). If you find that listening to particular songs makes you think about other people in sexual ways, you should junk the song. If you find yourself watching shows that are obsessed about sex, or include explicit sex scenes, you should turn the TV off. And if you find that you cannot even check your email without clicking through to porno sites, you should either bin your computer, or at least move it into a public place in your house like the living room that will make it very difficult to access such sites without your little sister blabbing to your mum.

When you start thinking about yourself and your boyfriend or girlfriend and you know you should aim for purity, but you still want to know how far you can go, here is my take for what it is worth. Try being Jesus-like rather than Pharisee-like about it. When I think about what's ok and what's not ok, and drawing sensible boundaries, for some strange reason I think of my two oldest sons. My eldest son James is a sensible person, almost too sensible for a kid. Sometimes I even call him Captain Sensible. Not in a million years would he play near the edge of a cliff. He is naturally cautious and has a spectator personality. So he'd probably enjoy watching other kids play near the edge of the cliff. He's a bit of a couch potato, so he would probably enjoy watching a video of other kids play near the edge of the cliff even more.

My younger son Ollie will go straight for the edge and will probably start running faster the closer he gets to it. Once on a camp I was talking to some parents for just a few minutes. James was happily throwing rocks at people's cars, pretty safe. But when I looked around for Ollie, I couldn't see him. I found him a hundred metres up the middle of the road, headed for the highway nearby.

Some people are like James when it comes to the physical side of dating relationships. You play it cautiously and carefully. In your aim for purity, some of you will decide not to kiss each other. This sounds uncommon, but it's actually a good and wise way to go. If your conscience tells you that it would be better to avoid kissing altogether, I would want to encourage you in that, not knock it, because you will not regret that decision. But most young people, even Christian ones, are more like Ollie, gleefully running towards danger. If that's you, you need to mark out some clear fences or boundaries a long way from danger, well away from the cliff of sexual immorality.

So some thoughts for the Ollies among us: if a guy is with a girl, he should not touch her breasts, her butt, or indeed any area that would ordinarily be covered by sensible underwear. I say 'sensible' because these days a couple of belt loops passes as underwear. If you are a guy and you are sleeping with a girl now, you should stop right now. A girl should never touch a guy's penis with anything (other than a taser in self-defence); it is simply a no-go zone that is off-limits before marriage. If you are a girl and you are in the habit of offering him oral sex, you should stop right now. Unlike what most people think these days, oral sex still counts as sex; the real giveaway is that it has the word 'sex' in it. And if you don't think you can stop, because you are doing these things with your boyfriend or girlfriend, then you actually should break up. Jesus said that it's better to undertake radical surgery so that you can go to heaven than to do nothing about sin and go to hell.

If you are going to kiss, then you must take responsibility for not letting it get overheated, or for even getting in a place where that can happen. Next time things get a bit too heated with your boyfriend or girlfriend, you should remind yourself that it will be much hotter in hell. That might help you get out of there fast. In terms of environments, don't let yourself be in a room with a closed door with your girlfriend or boyfriend. Don't let yourself be in any secluded place where there is not a good chance of someone interrupting you. Don't be home alone together. Don't be in a room with the lights out. If you are going to be alone, be somewhere where it would be totally normal and highly likely for someone else to walk past or to be able to see you. You need to go slow on the physical side of your relationships. In a U2 song called

'Original of the Species', Bono sings to his daughter:

> Baby slow down, the end is not as fun as the start
> Please stay a child somewhere in your heart.[3]

He just looks back on the experiences of his life and reckons that it's OK to go a little slow. Going slow on the physical side of dating relationships will breed obedience to God, and it will limit the genuine possibility of future regrets.

Two final words

Two final things are worth saying on this subject. Some people will actually go too far. They will make mistakes, race towards sexual immorality, not control their bodies, and take advantage of other people sexually. Many of us, in fact, will make mistakes in this area of the Christian life at some stage. It's very difficult not to when our bodies are raging with hormones and our society keeps shoving sexual messages down our throats each and every day. I'm not saying it's OK, and I'm not saying it's unavoidable. I'm just saying that many young Christians will make mistakes in their relationships.

So if that is you, you must realize that the consequences of our sexual decisions can be serious. 1 Thessalonians 4 says that the Lord will punish men for all such sins. Use that realization to drag you to your knees in repentance before Jesus. Don't let your heart turn hard. Turn back to Jesus, because forgiveness, redemption and the promise of no condemnation is on offer. The person and work of Jesus show us that God is the God of second chances, and third chances and fourth chances. He is the one who turns things around and who makes what is wrong right again. He certainly did that in the Thessalonians' lives, and he can do that in our lives too.

The other thing to mention is that some people are nowhere near making mistakes in this area. Maybe you've never had a boyfriend or girlfriend. That is OK; probably better in fact. It certainly doesn't make you less of a person, and it certainly frees you up to have lots of good friendships that will bring lots of good to you. It's better to have lots of good friends who are guys and girls, than lots of ex-boyfriends or ex-girlfriends. Almost all of the benefits of companionship that you get from a boyfriend or girlfriend, you can get from having lots of good friends of both genders. And it's cheaper, and is usually a lot less hassle, and you stand a much better chance of avoiding sexual immorality.

To finish up then, we can say that there is much more to safe sex than knowing how to use a condom. Although God is for sex and sexuality according to his design, he is against sexual immorality, in all its forms. He wants Christian people to avoid it, to learn to control their own bodies, and not to take advantage of one another. As Christian people we are bombarded with sexual messages, but this message from the Scriptures is clear enough. And that's why we should aim for purity in our dating relationships, and make clear boundaries that protect us from sexual immorality. And rather than obsessing about boyfriends and girlfriends, remember that good friendships are really good, and the forgiveness we all have in Jesus is even better.

CHAPTER 3

Is Jesus homophobic?

Faggot, fag, poofter, poof, queer, dyke, fairy, gay-boy; are these words in your vocabulary? Some of them turn up in mine from time to time, I have to concede, although in fairness, more out of laziness than malice. It's sometimes easier to call something 'gay' than look for a better descriptive word. But that's no excuse; these words have nevertheless made it into my vocabulary. Are they in yours?

We have already seen that our great God designed sex and sexuality to be explored and enjoyed within a binding covenant relationship between a man and a woman, which we call marriage. One of the questions that unbelievers might often (but not always) mockingly ask is why someone would wait until marriage before exploring sex. The other most common question young people ask is whether or not Jesus is homophobic. Or to put it another way, what is the Christian view of homosexuality?

Let's be honest here, it's not just unbelievers who are confused about the Christian view of homosexuality; many Christians are confused too. This is partly because there are ministers who claim to speak in the name of God who have bizarrely but openly said that homosexuals (along with other pagans, abortionists, feminists, etc.) must bear some blame for the suicide attacks on the World Trade Center on September 11, 2001.[4] Equally, in many parts of the world there are openly homosexual ministers and churches who keep the Bible's teaching about sexuality in the closet from which they themselves came out, and explain this away by saying in effect that Jesus was all about love. Some churches want to conduct gay marriages and even ordain gay priests. Other churches, it seems, would rather kill homosexuals. Some Christians march alongside homosexual people when they celebrate their homosexual lifestyle in the Gay and Lesbian Mardi Gras Parade held in Sydney every year. Other Christians turn up to the parade to protest with placards.

I'm not saying that the people who turn up to protest the Mardi Gras Parade are necessarily inappropriate, because the sustained witness of the Scriptures is that homosexual sex and a gay lifestyle are incompatible with God's design for humanity and sexuality. But the question is whether that is all there is to say on the Christian response to homosexuality.

Between liberal churches that want to ordain homosexual priests and Christian politicians who want to protest against the Mardi Gras, there are thousands of Christians who are pretty confused about what Jesus really thinks about homosexuality. You are probably one of them. Hopefully, not for much longer.

The origins and causes of homosexuality

Before we talk about the Bible's take on homosexuality, I want to quickly talk about possible origins or causes of homosexuality. But before we even do that we need to work out what we are talking about. Some people experience same-sex orientation, feelings and tendencies, which we might call *homosexual attraction*. When those feelings or attractions are acted upon sexually we are talking about homosexual practice or *homosexual sex*. When a person buys into the whole homosexual community, sub-culture and lifestyle, that is what we call *gay* (for dudes) or *lesbian* (for girls). So there can be people with *homosexual attraction* who never progress to *homosexual sex*. And there are people who progress to *homosexual sex* who do not buy into the *gay lifestyle*. And there are people who are happy and unhappy in each of those three categories. And that might even include you.

But what of the *causes* of homosexuality? Many will say that Christian opposition to homosexual sex and the gay lifestyle is stupid and unfair because people are born homosexual. It is often claimed or assumed these days that there is a genetic basis for homosexuality—what is sometimes called 'the gay gene'. But in fact there is no solid scientific support for the existence of the 'gay gene'. The 1994 Hamer study, which claimed to have found the gay gene, had a small sample size, and has been widely criticized. (Hamer was even investigated for scientific fraud over the study, although he was later cleared.) More importantly, his results have not been reproduced or replicated anywhere. In fact, two later studies have rejected Hamer's finding that some cases of homosexuality are linked to a particular gene.[5]

In 1991, an Australian study by Bailey and Pillard on identical twin brothers found that in only 50% of cases where homosexuality was identified in one brother, was it also there in the other brother, even though they shared the exact same genetic structure.[6] In itself this might suggest that factors other than genetics are more important in determining sexuality. However, this particular study was based upon sets of twin brothers who had been recruited by advertising in homosexual newspapers and magazines, rather than in periodicals intended for the general public. When Bailey and his colleagues conducted a similar study in 2000, but with twin brothers recruited from the Australian Twin Registry, the figure dropped from 50% to 20%.[7]

Gets you thinking, doesn't it? Gets you thinking that the guys putting out these studies might be more motivated by preconceived ideas or political agendas than by science.[8] Also gets you thinking that it must be something else in someone's upbringing other than their genetic make-up that explains their homosexual attraction or orientation.

A further challenge to the genetic basis for homosexual orientation is the idea that few homosexual people tend to have children. Given that very few homosexuals reproduce and have kids of their own, if homosexuality were inherited from parents genetically, then we would expect homosexuality to be rather quickly eliminated from the gene pool. So it seems very unlikely that there is any such thing as a 'gay gene'. But rather than using this information to go on the attack, I hope we can use it to speak with some degree of knowledge when we come to talk about a Christian approach to people struggling with homosexual orientation or practice.

But the thing is, just because someone isn't born homosexual, it doesn't mean that they necessarily choose homosexual attraction, sex or lifestyle in the same way that you might choose one ice-cream over another from the corner store. It may well be that experiences in a person's life shape their sexuality. For example, it can arise in males in the absence of an older and involved male in a boy's development. If a boy never got any attention from his dad, he might look for affection and attention from other older males, which becomes sexualized during teenage years with the onset of puberty. It is in fact quite common for people in puberty to have some homosexual thoughts or feelings which pass without ever developing further. So if you have strange thoughts or feelings, that doesn't mean you are 'gay'. It may well pass.

Homosexuality might also be the result of some physical or sexual abuse during childhood years. This is apparently an important factor in homosexual women, for whom the lesbian lifestyle can be as much a choice against men as it is an irresistible attraction to women.

The other massive origin of homosexuality is external labelling.

A boy or a girl is a little different from his or her peers and is labelled by them a 'gay-boy' or (in the case of a girl) a 'tomboy'. As Dr George O'Malley from TV's *Grey's Anatomy* said, "High school sucks if you are even a little bit different from everyone else". George was simply saying that if you happen to stand out from the crowd during your teenage years, get used to people giving you a hard time and calling you names. The problem is that sometimes you can start believing some of those names, and that's external labelling. Imagine a 12-year-old boy who is really into ballet. It doesn't just happen in *Billy Elliot*; it also happens to real people. If a 12-year-old boy is into moving his body to music in ballet rather than kicking a ball around a paddock, you know that he is going to get hammered in high school. That is external labelling, and I reckon that Christian young people in schools, colleges and workplaces should do their best to protect people in those situations from copping abuse day in and out.

What does the Bible say about homosexuality?

We have already seen from the Bible that God designed sex to be between a man and a woman. No suitable companion for the first man Adam could be found from among the animals. And so in Genesis 2, God made a woman from the man. Some would say it was an improvement; others would say, "What could you expect from a spare rib?" But putting lame feminist and chauvinist jokes aside, what is clear is that God did not make another man from the sleeping Adam; he made a woman. In the beginning, the woman and the man were built for each other. That's kind of obvious if you think of the male and female bodies—they just fit together. But according to the opening chapters of the Bible, the fit is more than physical and sexual; it is deeply emotional and spiritual too. The Old Testament affirms this fit or design in places such as Malachi 2, and both Jesus and the Apostle Paul also honour it in Matthew 5:32, Matthew 19:5, 1 Corinthians 6:16 and Ephesians 5:31.

If Genesis 2 tells us that a binding relationship between a man and a woman is God's design for humanity and sexuality, it is not surprising to also find that God dislikes homosexual sex intensely. In the Old Testament, we see this in places like Leviticus 18:22, and in the New Testament in places like Romans 1. Notice that I said that God dislikes *homosexual sex*—I have not said anything about *homosexual attraction*. If someone with homosexual attraction decides not to dwell upon homosexual thoughts or not to act on their attraction by having homosexual sex, I want to encourage them with their struggle against sin. In the Bible, God clearly states that he hates homosexual sex.

That doesn't mean the Bible is silent on homosexual attraction. If someone were to have homosexual feelings or attraction, that person can train his or her mind for righteousness, just as people with immoral heterosexual feelings can also train their minds for righteousness. The same things we said last chapter about training our minds for righteousness also apply here.

But to sum up, the Bible clearly speaks against homosexual sex and instructs us all to train our minds for righteousness rather than fuel immoral sexual feelings or attraction, whether they are homosexual or heterosexual.

The gospel to homosexuals

As God is a God of grace, these are not the final words of the Scriptures on this matter. Perhaps the best place to go is 1 Corinthians 6:9-11, which has been described as the 'gospel to homosexuals':

Do you not know that the wicked will not inherit the kingdom of God? Do not be deceived: Neither the sexually immoral nor idolaters nor adulterers nor male prostitutes nor homosexual offenders nor thieves nor the greedy nor drunkards nor slanderers nor swindlers will inherit the kingdom of God. And that is what some of you were. But you were washed, you were sanctified, you were justified in the name of the Lord Jesus Christ and by the Spirit of our God.

These are huge verses and I reckon we can learn crucial things from them. The first is that our sexual activity can jeopardise our eternity. It's not just a matter of personal preference (as the gay lobby often tells us). Our sexual actions can jeopardise our eternities. The wicked will not inherit the kingdom of God, nor the sexually immoral, nor adulterers, nor male prostitutes, nor homosexual offenders. Our sexual activity is important because it has consequences for this life and the next.

But the second thing we learn here is that homosexual sex is not a worse category of sin than any others. We know that God hates homosexual sin because it falls short of his great design for sex, but he hates all kinds of sexual immorality. This includes adultery, when a married person has sex with someone whom they are not married to; or fornication, when two unmarried people have sex; or incest, when two close family members have sex; or (in my view) the unrepentant viewing of pornography. It's not like the dude who is having sex with his boyfriend is any worse than the married dude who is having sex with a woman who is not his wife, or the (unmarried) boyfriend and girlfriend who are sleeping together. But here is the amazing and humbling thing: God also hates theft and greed, and drunkenness and slander, and lies and cons. If you recognize yourself in anything on that list, like I do, that should keep you from thinking that you are better than the homosexual sinner.

The third and most amazing thing we read is that change is possible. As the Apostle Paul, Jesus' official spokesman, looks at that list of vices, and as he looks at the people in the church at Corinth, he can say (past tense): "and that is what some of you *were*" (1 Cor 6:11). That is what they were, he says, but something radical happened when they put their trust in the death and resurrection of Jesus Christ. Because although they used to practice homosexual sex or steal or slander, they were *washed* of their sins. They were no longer stained by the evil things they had previously done. Although they used to be adulterers or male prostitutes, they were *sanctified*—that is, set apart for God's purposes and holy living. Although they previously practised unnatural and unrighteous sex or swindled people out of their money with lies, now they were *justified*—that is, declared righteous in the name of Jesus by the power of the Holy Spirit. That is what they *were*, but Jesus changed them. Change is possible.

Which is not to say that the instant you trust in Jesus you never face the temptation to act upon same-sex attraction, or whatever happens to be the temptation you battle with, ever again. But it is to say that change is possible. Because every person—homosexual, adulterer, greedy person, you, me—who trusts in Jesus now has a choice. And that choice is whether to live by your own feelings and experiences and act upon them, or to surrender your life to Jesus and live according to God's word, in spite of those feelings and experiences. Change is possible, even for homosexual people. That is what some of you were, says Paul to the Corinthians.

With the help of the Holy Spirit, and fellow believers, a person can change their identity so that it is no longer found in the gay or lesbian lifestyle, but in relationship with Jesus. With the help of the Spirit, homosexual people can change their behaviour so that they move on from acting out same-sex desires. And with the help of the Spirit a person can even change their desires so that same sex desires are less overwhelming and compulsive. Christians working in ministries that support people struggling with same-sex attraction disagree about whether it is helpful for people to aim to move towards heterosexual attraction. Some consider this to be the goal for repentant Christians battling same-sex attraction; others think it breeds false hope that can be destructive. But the good news remains good news: there is hope and healing for people who struggle with homosexual sex and same-sex attraction. One of them says:

> People may have little option about their starting point, but they have great choice about their final destination.[9]

Help where help is needed

Change is possible—that is good news for young Christians struggling with homosexual attraction. But there is also good news for young Christians who in God's good grace don't have this particular struggle. And that is that you can help where help is needed. Change is not only possible for homosexual Christians, but it can be supported, encouraged and nurtured by fellow Christians.

The starting point is to be open enough to talk about homosexuality without making all the usual lame jokes. It will also help to recognize that homosexual attraction is a genuine struggle that will affect people in our schools, colleges, workplaces, churches and youth groups, and to not place homosexual sex in a worse category of sin than all the other sins we struggle with. We should all admit that genuine struggle with sin is the norm in the Christian life, and that it is there in every Christian's life, somewhere, if we are honest enough. Openly acknowledging this gives Christian brothers and sisters the permission they need to do the Christian thing and struggle on.

We can also take a lead role in protecting those people who might be just that little bit different. We can protect them from that external labelling—by not contributing to it, but also by defending them from it. I remember when I was at school there was a guy in my class who was a little bit different. I can't imagine what it was like for him to go to school every day. But I can imagine what it was like for him to go on our school adventure camp every year, because he always ended up in our tent on account of no-one else being willing to have him. Every night, over and over again, the 'tough' guys would creep out and pull down our tent, just because the slightly different dude was in it. I remember it being a real pain, but looking back I am glad that it was the Christians in my class who gave this guy a home and a measure of protection for what must have been a hell of a week for him. I once hit a kid in the year above me at school when he was taunting this guy with homosexual jibes. My youth leaders reckoned it was a terrible thing to do, but looking back I think I should have done more to protect him. In little and big ways, we can play a pretty important part in being friends, protectors and safe harbours for people in our schools and teams and churches and clubs who are just that little bit different. That strikes me as a Christian kind of thing to do.

We've covered a lot of territory in this chapter, so it might help to bring it all together. We remembered the Bible's insistence that sex is between a man and a woman, bound to each other for the long haul. That is Scripture's constant witness, and we do people who struggle with homosexuality no favours by going soft on that. We recognized that the Christian life is incompatible with a gay and lesbian lifestyle, but we also saw that although people aren't genetically gay, they most likely didn't choose to be homosexual either. And we learned most importantly that even if people struggling with homosexual issues have little choice about their starting point, they do have choice about their final destination. And so for those who want to change in obedience to Jesus and with the help of the Holy Spirit, we as fellow sinners and recipients of God's grace must support them.

CHAPTER 4

Pornography and lust

I remember the first time I saw pictures of a naked woman. I was about nine years old and was mucking around in the bush across the road from my house with some of my buddies. We stumbled across someone's stash of *Penthouse* magazines and started looking through them with a fair bit of intrigue and a little bit of embarrassment. My first thought was that the ladies in the magazines must be pretty cold without any clothes on.

A couple of years later, my friends and I had a secret cubby house in the bush, and one of my mates brought along a *Playboy* magazine that he had nicked from his dad. Being just a little bit older than the previous time, it didn't occur to me that the naked women were cold. I just thought they were beautiful and it all seemed pretty harmless. That's the sort of view that lots of people have about pornography—that it is really just harmless pictures of naked beautiful people who don't feel the cold.

According to a recent study, 97% of girls and 100% of boys had seen porn by the time they turned 15.[10] The same study found that teenagers were getting most of their information about sex from internet pornography sites rather than from their parents or sex education programs. Though those figures look very high, you might think that if it just means that every boy has stumbled across a stash of magazines with pictures of naked ladies by the time he's turned 15, that's not so alarming.

But there is good reason to be alarmed, because pornography and the attendant problems it creates is a rapidly growing phenomenon, as tracked by Mark Driscoll in his booklet *Porn Again Christian: A Frank Discussion of Pornography and Masturbation*:

- In the 1950s, no stores carried soft pornography.
- In the 1960s, *Playboy* was made available behind the counter.
- In the 1970s, *Penthouse* made it next to *Playboy* on the shelf.[11]
- Since the 1990s, every form of sexual encounter and perversion imaginable has been documented on an estimated one million porn sites on the internet.

Within just two generations we have gone from one magazine

under the counter to a practically limitless supply. Figures suggest up to 1000 new porn sites are created every day.

But the problem is not only that there has been a massive increase in the amount of pornography available. The problem is not even that you don't have to rack up the courage to go into a newsagent to get your hands on it. The problem is that you can view whatever you want from the privacy of your own room through the internet. The added problem is that the porn available is getting increasingly graphic and violent and our society is rapidly becoming desensitized to all but the very worst on offer.[12] Images that appear in mainstream men's and women's magazines today were saved for only the most risqué and scandalous of magazines of yesterday. We have become used to softer forms of pornography, and so our society as a whole has moved to more violent and graphic forms. And sadly, there seems to be a great market for it, even among Christian people.

For our purposes, we will consider lust and pornography together because they are closely linked. It is notoriously difficult to define pornography, but as an American Supreme Court Judge said nearly half a century ago, "We know it when we see it".[13] Lust can be defined as something like a strong sexual desire for someone or something that is not yours to have, often fuelled by the eyes. The lust of human eyes is partly responsible for bringing sin into the world. At the devil's prompting, Eve saw that the forbidden fruit in the garden of Eden was good for food and pleasing to the eye and also desirable for gaining knowledge—and so she took it, even though it was not hers to take. The Apostle John, probably Jesus' best earthly friend, tells us that the lust of sinful man's eyes doesn't come from God but from the world opposed to God (1 John 2:16). But when we are talking about lust in this chapter, we are especially talking about sexual lust: the immoral desiring of another person's body.

This does not mean that it is wrong to notice that another person is physically attractive. Noticing that someone is attractive at a first glance is not lust, but a lingering second look is starting to get closer, and undressing the person in your mind is all the way there. This understanding of lust means that it is not sinful for a husband to have a strong sexual desire for his wife, and vice versa, but it does mean that it is sinful for him to have sexual desire for any other woman.

We will discuss lust and pornography together because it is very difficult to look at pornography and not to lust. The whole point of pornography is lust. And given the statistics above, it is clear that lusting is fuelled by high rates of pornography use, particularly internet pornography use among young people.

One approach to dealing with pornography and pornographic lust is simply to condemn it outright. Job, the wisest man of ancient times, tells how he made a covenant *with his eyes* not to look lustfully at a girl (Job 31:1). And Jesus tells his followers to take the radical surgical action of plucking out their eyes if their eyes cause them to sin (the emphasis is on the radical action rather than the literal surgery of gouging out your eye; Matt 18:9). What's good enough for Job and good enough for Jesus is good enough for us, so you might think the best approach is just to outlaw porn altogether, and to tell everyone to STOP IT!

But because porn has such a powerful influence over young people, simply saying STOP IT might make young people just desire it all the more. As well as condemning lust as Jesus does, and aiming for purity as Job does, it might help if we take some time to understand why pornography is damaging—why it is definitely not as harmless as it seems. There is something quite sinister lurking beneath what might appear to be harmless; something that damages both the people in the pictures and those who are looking at them.

Damaging the people looking at the pictures

Even at its absolute best, pornography teaches young boys and girls to view other people as a collection of body parts separate from who they are as people. Young men in particular quickly learn from pornography that women are little more than physical objects existing purely for their viewing and doing pleasure. A woman then becomes the sum of her breasts, legs, butt and vagina, rather than someone made in the image of God, which the opening chapter of the Bible tells us that all people are.

You don't need to be a genius to work out that this is going to hugely distort a young man's view of women. He will learn to think of women basically as pieces of meat for his own sexual fantasy and pleasure. Feminist author Naomi Wolf believes that when men get too accustomed to the unrealistic, photo-shopped women in porn, 'real' women become 'just bad porn' rather than creatures of sublime physical and spiritual beauty and complexity. Incredibly, this non-Christian writer who has been at the forefront of liberating women's sexuality for decades said, "I am noting that the power and charge of sex are maintained when there is some sacredness to it, when it is not on tap all the time".[14] At the most extreme end, prolonged exposure to pornographic material can lead otherwise normal young men to become violent and/or sexual predators.[15]

Mark Kastleman has been researching the effects of pornography for over a decade, and has discovered that pornography causes chemical alterations in the brain that affect attitudes and behaviour in teenagers and adults.[16] In other words, porn literally and biologically messes with your head. It also messes with a young man's view of masculinity and male sexuality. Instead of being a provider for and a protector of the women in his life, he quickly learns that being a man means taking what you want from women with no care for them and no responsibility towards them. It further warps a young man's view of his own sexuality, as sexuality turns into a quick sexual release in response to a woman on a screen who, though she appears inviting, remains a picture on a screen. And when a young man does that he sells himself well short of what God has in store for him—which is a deeply spiritual and physical union between a man and a woman who have committed themselves to one another for life. The naked woman on the screen only loves him until he has had sexual release; then she mocks him, scorns him and despises him. The excitement which dresses itself up as romance and intimacy is smashed by the shame he feels towards himself and the stain on his own soul. It's pretty hard to downplay the damage that pornography does to the people looking at the pictures. Young men (and women as well) would do well to put into practice what Job and Jesus so clearly said. Too much is at stake to do otherwise.

Damaging the people in the pictures

But pornography and the lust that is fuelled by it does not just damage the people looking at the porn. It also damages the people in the pictures. Not many people ever think about the issue of pornography and lust from this point of view. But the pornography industry, supported by the people who view it, is responsible for scarring so many of the people in it. It may appear that the models and actors in the pictures and videos are having a jolly old time, but you never get to hear how they feel about it when the camera is turned off.

It is virtually impossible to find statistics on the matter, but anecdotes suggest that many of the women involved in porn were sexually assaulted when they were young. Additionally, many of the women in pornographic magazines and websites are trapped in sexual slavery. That is, they have little choice but to perform what were previously unspeakable acts, for the viewing pleasure of porno users. Many do not choose to enter the pornography industry but are lured into it by deception and false pretence. They are not free to choose what they will and will not do, and they are not free to leave the industry or their 'employers'. Others are enslaved to drug habits that can only be supported by prostitution or porn acting funded by viewers at their computer screens. Many get completely stoned or take painkillers so that they can withstand the physical trauma that is dealt to them. No doubt some of the models and actors enjoy their work, or at least the notoriety that is attached to it. But the cold reality is that everyone in the pictures is being scarred, and a majority of them know it only too well. This should make young people think twice before they turn on their computer, or buy an X-rated video by mail order, or do whatever they do to get their hands on material that so deeply scars the daughters of Eve.

Whether it is simply viewing naked people or committing violent crimes it is straightforward enough to say that pornography in the internet age is far from harmless. It damages the people watching and it damages the people being watched. And God wants better things for all those people.

What to do with it

Hopefully by this stage we can agree that lust and pornography are far removed from the way God intended humans to express their sexuality. Sometimes he really must be shaking his head up there in heaven. But the question is: What should we do with it all? Because, sadly, the world we live in and know so well is full of pornography.

One option would be just to ignore the problem. Unfortunately, this seems to be the preferred option of many parents, with their kids battling pornography addiction under their rooves thanks to broadband connections and multiple computers paid for with their credit cards. Ignorance looks like a pretty bad option. If we were to ask the question 'What Would Jesus Do with pornography?' one thing we know for sure is that he wouldn't do nothing. Doing nothing is not the answer.

The first part of the answer is to tell yourself often who you are in Christ Jesus. Real, lasting, inside-out change must start from the inside, with the knowledge that God has made you, that Jesus loves you and that the Holy Spirit wants to work in you. Remind yourself that you are neither helpless nor a fool: Jesus has rescued you from sin, and God has given you everything you need for life and godliness. You might even want to stick a note with something like this written on it right next to your computer screen.

Once you are armed with the deep spiritual knowledge of who you are in Christ Jesus, decisive action is required, particularly when you consider how easily viewing pornography goes from being an interest to being an obsession to being an uncontrollable addiction.[17] The Bible clearly states that God doesn't want us to be mastered or controlled by anything other than his word and his Spirit (1 Cor 6:12). Even though internet pornography wasn't around when 1 Corinthians was written, it is still covered by this instruction. Renowned Christian psychologist Dr Archibald Hart says:

> It's important to remind yourself that you have a choice when it comes to behaviour. You can break the habit gradually or go cold turkey and stop it all at once. I think cold turkey is best for this addiction. Gradual never works because it keeps the exposure going.[18]

Perhaps the very first thing a young man or woman should do with pornography is to get rid of it all. Junk any magazines; they're not even worthy of recycling. Do the same with any secret stash of movies you might have. Delete all the pictures and videos and bookmarks that you have hidden on your computer. Delete any pictures you have on your phones and iPods, and get rid of any movies you might have that might be pretty mainstream but have porno scenes in them.

But you will also want to get rid of future opportunities to view pornography or fuel porno lust. So move any computers and TVs out of your bedroom and into common rooms or high-traffic areas in your house. If it is your habit to view pornography at home before your parents get home from work, see if you can stay back later at school or university or work. You could even ask your parents to switch some of their work arrangements around so that at least someone else is at home when you get home. You will probably need to have an honest chat with your folks for this to work, which will seem like the most awkward thing in the world to do, so it may not happen for everyone. But you could always try talking to a parent when you are driving in the car somewhere, just the two of you. That might minimize some of the awkwardness, especially if you ease your way into the conversation. Just blurting out that you have been watching people have sex on their computer might cause a car accident if you don't first let them know that you need to talk to them about something serious and important to you.

Website accountability software, which sends a list of websites that you have accessed from your computer to someone else, is also available. It would be a good idea to set this up with a trusted older person or leader rather than just your mates. Covenant Eyes, which has been developed by Christians in the US, provides very detailed reports on a timely basis (www.covenanteyes.com). X3watch (www.xxxchurch.com) does pretty much the same thing, although it is probably worth paying for the professional edition, as the free edition is unsupported.

Getting professional counselling from a reputable Christian psychologist or counsellor is another good option to be pursued when the options above do not prove effective in breaking an interest, obsession or addiction to pornography. Of course, there are counsellors and there are counsellors, so you want to make sure that your counsellor doesn't only call themselves a Christian but can demonstrate to you how they apply their Christianity and the Bible to their counselling work.

Dr Archibald Hart's words (on page 65) seem to me to be the place to end our discussion of pornography and pornographic lust.

I really like the way he said we have a choice when it comes to behaviour—and that means we don't have to be helpless victims of pornography. I also really like it because God says it too. The Bible tells us that by God's grace we can put to death our sin and be alive to Jesus. Most of the young people I talk with about pornography carry on as though they are helpless victims who have no option but to give into the urge to view porn. But surely Jesus Christ did not die so that we would be caught in a never-ending trap of lust. Surely when he triumphed over evil on the cross, that included the evil of pornography. Surely the Holy Spirit can enable us to steer ourselves away from this temptation. Surely the grace of God can teach us to say no to this particular ungodliness. Surely God is refining our hearts so that his sons can be the very glory of God as they are described in the New Testament, rather than puppets who themselves prop up an industry that brings so much harm to others and to themselves.

If you are feeling guilt and shame over pornographic lust, don't forget that there is no condemnation for those who are in Christ Jesus. Don't forget that God delights in his children, rejoicing over them with singing in their good moments and quietening and forgiving them in his love in the bad moments. Bring your guilt and shame to the cross and deal with it there, at the place God has provided.

The only outcome that would be worse than living in guilt and shame would be if you put this book down and continued to feel like an addict or a victim. The grace of God has appeared in Jesus. It has brought us salvation, and it teaches us to say "No" to ungodliness and to say "Yes" to Jesus. You may need help in your journey of saying no to ungodliness, but you are no helpless victim.

Sex on your own

Before we finish a book called *Sex* we should say something about masturbation, given that it is the most common sexual practice among young people. It's a pretty tricky subject to talk about because there's some serious difference of opinion on it, and because it's usually associated with shame. As the quirky American film director Woody Allen said, "The only difference between sex and death is, with death you can do it alone and nobody's going to make fun of you". Mind you, Woody Allen also said, "Don't knock masturbation—it's sex with someone I love", so perhaps we're better off getting someone else's advice on masturbation.

You might be interested to discover that the Bible says nothing specific about masturbation. Some people think there are a couple of Old Testament references to it, but those passages are talking about other things. The Bible talks about lots of other sexual practices that are against God's will, including sex with animals, but masturbation is never mentioned. This means that we cannot condemn masturbation outright, nor endorse it, because Scripture is silent on the issue.

However, as we've seen already, the Bible is not at all silent on the issue of lust and sexual purity. Lust is very clearly against the will of God, and so any masturbation that involves or includes lust should be repented of and avoided. We've included discussion of masturbation in this chapter on pornography because, for many people, lust, pornography and masturbation cannot be separated; they're all part of the one activity. So certainly masturbation that is connected to lust and pornography is something to combat in your personal life. It requires taking action just as radical as for other things we have talked about in this book.

But, you might say, what about masturbation that doesn't include lustful thoughts and fantasies? If the Bible doesn't condemn it, does that make it okay?

Well, first off let's just acknowledge that this supposed form of 'pure' masturbation is not all that common! Masturbation very often goes along with impure, lustful thoughts, and if you make a habit of masturbating then it is almost certain that you also make a habit of thinking lustfully and impurely about other people, and probably people you know. To develop a habit of masturbation is, in my view, a foolish and hypocritical thing for a Christian to do. You can't pray "Lead us not into temptation" and then masturbate regularly.

It's also pretty obvious that masturbation is not God's design for human sexuality. As we've seen already, God designed sex to be between a man and a woman within a covenantal marriage relationship. Masturbation is hardly that. It's sex on your own; it's not the ideal.

Having said all that, if it can be done without the temptation to lust, then I would suggest (very tentatively) that masturbation could be a permissible way to allow for the occasional release of pent-up sexual urges. I say this very cautiously, because I don't want this to be read as an encouragement to begin or continue the practice of masturbation. But I also don't want young people to suffer under years of considerable guilt about something on which the Bible is basically silent.

Conclusion

We started this book by wondering if there was a positive view of sex that rises above thinking of sex as just the casual answer to a physical need. I guess it would be a shame, then, to finish a positive quest with a chapter on pornography, perhaps the biggest sexual blight of our time.

Let me remind you then of what we have discovered: that sex is one of God's great gifts to humanity. It is beautiful and hot and earthy and very good, but like all his gifts it can be used well or abused mightily, which is why this book has been so up front about some of the mistakes that young people can make. I've also been up front about listening to what God says about his gift—in particular about where and how to use it (in marriage). My hope and prayer is that you will honour the Lord Jesus Christ with your body and your sexuality, and that in time you will experience this wonderful gift for yourself, free from shame and regret, and full of joy and pleasure.

Feedback on this resource

We really appreciate getting feedback about our resources—not just suggestions for how to improve them, but also positive feedback and ways they can be used. We especially love to hear that the resources may have helped someone in their Christian growth.

You can send feedback to us via the 'Feedback' menu in our online store, or write to us at PO Box 225, Kingsford NSW 2032, Australia.

Endnotes

1. R Williams, S Duffy and C Heath, 'Sin Sin Sin', from the album *Intensive Care*, BMG, Hollywood Hills, 2005.
2. L Waite and M Gallagher, *The Case for Marriage: Why Married People are Happier, Healthier and Better Off Financially*, Broadway Books, New York, 2001.
3. U2, 'Original of the Species', from the album *How to Dismantle an Atomic Bomb*, Universal-Island, Dublin, 2004.
4. On 13 September 2001, television evangelists Jerry Falwell and Pat Robertson, two of the most prominent voices of the religious right, said liberal civil liberties groups, feminists, homosexuals and abortion rights supporters bore partial responsibility for terrorist attacks because their actions lifted the curtain of God's protection and turned God's anger against America.
5. DH Hamer et al., 'A linkage between DNA markers on the X chromosome and male sexual orientation', *Science*, vol. 261, no. 5119, 16 July 1993, p. 321. Also see Dean Hamer's book, *The Science of Desire: The Search for the Gay Gene and the Biology of Behavior*, Simon & Schuster, New York, 1994. Critiques of Hamer's study and the general notion that there is a gay gene are available from sources such as the National Association

for Research and Therapy of Homosexuality (www.narth.com). From within the scientific community itself, Drs George Rice and George Ebers of the University of Western Ontario and Stanford University tried to replicate Hamer's chromosomal results in their study in April 1999. Rice and Ebers could not and concluded that their "… results do not support an X-linked gene underlying male homosexuality". Rice et al., 'Male homosexuality: absence of linkage to microsatellite markers at xq28', *Science*, vol. 284, no. 5414, 23 April 1999, p. 665.

6. JM Bailey and RC Pillard, 'A genetic study of male sexual orientation', *Archives of General Psychiatry*, vol. 48, no. 12, December 1991, pp. 1089-96.

7. Bailey and his research buddies admitted it is very difficult to distinguish the genetic from the environmental influences on sexual orientation. See JM Bailey, MP Dunne and NG Martin, 'Genetic and environmental influences on sexual orientation and its correlates in an Australian twin sample', *Journal of Personality and Social Psychology*, vol. 78, no. 3, March 2000, pp. 524-36.

8. Despite much media hype about 'gay genes', no-one has ever proved a biological cause for homosexuality. Every case in which someone has claimed to discover a biological cause for homosexuality has been discredited when their research has come under the scrutiny of 'non-gay' scientists. The media tends to give a lot more exposure to the initial 'discoveries' than they do to the debunking of those discoveries. Many

of the authors have been part of the politically active gay lobby. For example, after publishing his now thoroughly discredited study on 'gay brains', researcher Simon LeVay went on to open a school for 'gay' studies.

9. I heard Chris Keane say this. Chris is the author of *What Some of You Were* (Matthias Media, Sydney, 2001), and helped set up Liberty Christian Ministries to provide support, hope and education to Christian men and women (and their families, spouses and friends) who experience unwanted same-sex attraction. See www.libertychristianministries.org.au.

10. Reported in *Sex Lives of Australian Teenagers* (Random House Australia, North Sydney, 2007), by Joan Sauers. The results were based on an online survey of 300 Australian teenagers.

11. Mark Driscoll, *Porn-Again Christian*, Re:Lit, Mars Hill, 2009, p. 12.

12. This is not just anecdotal or observation. A study prepared by the American Psychological Association reported that men exposed long-term to pornography and/or sexual violence linked to pornography in the media "become desensitized to violence and are less sympathetic to rape victims". See Dr Archibald Hart, *The Sexual Man: Masculinity without Guilt*, Thomas Nelson Publishing, 1995, p. 90, quoting the *Summary Report of the American Psychological Association Commission on Violence and Youth*, vol. 1, *Violence and Youth: Psychology's response*, American Psychological Association, Washington DC, November 1993. Startlingly, this study was prepared in November 1993, several years

before the internet took off in the public imagination and usage.

13. US Supreme Court Justice Stewart Potter, concurring opinion in *Jacobellis v. Ohio* 378 US (1964) at 184.

14. Nick Galvin, 'The porn ultimatum', *The Sydney Morning Herald*, 5 March 2009, quoting Naomi Wolf, 'The Porn Myth', *New York Magazine*, 20 October 2003.

15. For a chilling reality check, you could read the chapter on executed sexual predator and serial killer Ted Bundy in Driscoll's *Porn-Again Christian*.

16. See Mark Kastleman, *The Drug of the New Millennium: The Brain Science Behind Internet Pornography Use*, PowerThink Publishing, 2007.

17. Although some secular commentators do not want to treat pornography as addictive in the same way that alcohol and drugs are addictive, Kastleman's research suggests that pornography has a similar affect to alcohol and narcotics in terms of altering the chemical responses in the human brain.

18. Dr Archibald Hart, *The Sexual Man*, p. 97.

matthiasmedia

Matthias Media is an evangelical publishing ministry that seeks to persuade all Christians of the truth of God's purposes in Jesus Christ as revealed in the Bible, and equip them with high-quality resources, so that by the work of the Holy Spirit they will:

- abandon their lives to the honour and service of Christ in daily holiness and decision-making
- pray constantly in Christ's name for the fruitfulness and growth of his gospel
- speak the Bible's life-changing word whenever and however they can—in the home, in the world and in the fellowship of his people.

To find out more about our large range of very useful resources, and to access samples and free downloads, visit our website:

www.matthiasmedia.com.au

How to buy our resources

1. Direct from us over the internet:
   – in the US: www.matthiasmedia.com
   – in Australia and the rest of the world:
     www.matthiasmedia.com.au

2. Direct from us by phone:
   – in the US: 1 866 407 4530
   – in Australia: 1800 814 360 (Sydney: 9663 1478)
   – international: +61-2-9663-1478

> Register at our website for our **free** regular email update to receive information about the latest new resources, **exclusive special offers**, and free articles to help you grow in your Christian life and ministry.

3. Through a range of outlets in various parts of the world.
   Visit **www.matthiasmedia.com.au/information/contact-us** for details about recommended retailers in your part of the world, including www.thegoodbook.co.uk in the United Kingdom.

4. Trade enquiries can be addressed to:
   – in the US and Canada: sales@matthiasmedia.com
   – in Australia and the rest of the world: sales@matthiasmedia.com.au

predestination

Have you ever wondered whether God gave Adam and Eve free will? Or what 'free will' even means?

Have you ever wondered whether God influences us to make the decisions we make day to day? And if he does, how exactly he does it?

Have you ever wanted to know what the Bible means when it says some are chosen or predestined? Is that good news or bad news for us?

If you have been a Christian for any length of time, you have probably wondered about these questions. In this Little Black Book on predestination, Scott Petty brings his trademark humour and clarity to a topic Christians often get tied in knots about.

FOR MORE INFORMATION OR TO ORDER CONTACT:

Matthias Media
Telephone: +61-2-9663-1478
Facsimile: +61-2-9663-3265
Email: sales@matthiasmedia.com.au
www.matthiasmedia.com.au

Matthias Media (USA)
Telephone: 1-866-407-4530
Facsimile: 724-964-8166
Email: sales@matthiasmedia.com
www.matthiasmedia.com